also by **joseph granda-padron**
available from **lulu press**

Abstraction (2005)

Veneer (2005)

Joseph Granda-Padron

OMEGA

First Lulu Press edition published in 2007

ISBN 0-6151-4158-9

This collection is dedicated to

Savage

"You know who you are, Brother.
They don't make 'em like you no
more.
Heart of gold and strong enough to
hold up the world!"

To have begun is to have done
half the task; dare to be wise.

—Horace

OMEGA

Anal

A moment of blessed
Calm. Serenity, bliss
And what-not all rolled
Into a single second
Of realization.
This is what you work
So hard
For, what you slave
To attain.
Mere seconds
Of peace, passion-calm.

(Looking down at her hips
the arc of her back
his hands firmly clasping
each of her ripe buttocks
feeling the will
to continue his pace
his withholding of release
he pushed on.
Deeper.
Deeper into her.
Deeper into himself.)

This is what you are
What you've always wanted.
She turns, looks at you
Working her and the beads
Of sweat spotting her
Forehead
Fill you with animosity
You must continue
You must hold sway
Over yourself
As to prolong this moment

This ecstasy
Of a second.

When she moans out
In pleasure you reach down
Feel the luscious strands
Of her young hair love
Your fingers and push
Her face into the mattress.
You're paying for this
Like you do every
Tuesday
Of every-every week
Things will go your way
Like it or not.

(Holding her head down
buffeting the predicted shouts
of pain
in one swift motion
he removed himself from
her cunt
and
shoved into her rectum.)

You hear
The muffled screams
Of her buried face
Turn slightly to maintain balance
And hold firm your position
As she struggles, knowing
This is what you saved yourself
For.
This purchasable agony
This final act
Of dominance / deliverance
Is your addiction.

(As he finishes
leaving her used body
twitching in pain tears
streaming in mascara-bliss
down her face, moans
emanating ever so pitifully

from her mouth
and hands
tightly clenching one another
he knew
broken condom and all
this is what he
paid for.)

You stand over her flesh
Swimming in pride
Engulfed in the seconds
You tower with throbbing
Completion.
The sweat of your body
Masking with fatigue
The true joy you feel
From your action.
This is where they all belong
Quivering / trembling
In pain.
PRAYING that it doesn't happen again
And again
But knowing that if it did
Resistance would prove
Heightened
Pleasure.

Avarice

Part one

Oh! The Flesh…
The skin and organs and limbs
Food can't quench this hunger.
Love neither.
This hunger is pure passion, pure sex, pure
            Nothing else.
Predator with eyes of desire we know.
Your clothing has no power of concealment
Clothing… only feeds the fire.

And my fire only consumes lust
It's never satisfied, never full, never
            Forgiving.
I've consumed the flesh, devoured it, drowned
            My loins in the sweet nectar of sinew.
I've bit, sucked, choked, restricted, strangled, toyed,
            Fucked, licked clean, and the hunger…

I want more.
I always want more.
Positions don't matter.
Orgasm stands as the least of worries.
My craving is the act; Pushing, pushing,

Pushing, PUSHING,
Over and over and over and the world
  Could line up in front of me.
  Plead with me, assume my conclusion.
Finished,
  A broken humanity at my feet, looking up to me,
  I'd say:
  "I'm ready for seconds!"

Part two

A master with hands, manipulation
Hours and hours of exercise the way you deserve,
The way you want and nothing of dissatisfaction.
Up, down, hard, rough, soft, satisfaction
There's a dragon in your hand called traction.
You beat and rub like it's a new fashion.

Why wait for flesh when you possess
All the possibilities of enlightenment in your hand?
God given enlightenment in your palm
Fingers blessed with fire, with compulsion.
Bang, pow, and there, you've released the magic lotion
You're calm.

Touch and go
It's there about to happen.
Stop. Let it go. Don't touch it!

Can't finish, now. Gotta keep going for as long as
Forever and ever and if it should happen
If conclusion should occur, the big finale…
Two minutes flat and we'll be back
At it again like old friends
That have been parted an eternity
Hand speeds bordering insanity.

The parts never fail, never stagger
Their always capable, workable
And when eternity explodes Viagra
With a grin and orgasm I'll be unstoppable.

Part Three

But flesh has no meaning when all one wants is solitude.
Walk the road of life and pain a loner
Without care or baggage,
Regard or alliance.

No one standing at the finish line to see me triumph.
No one to boost my spirits when I'm in a slump.
Dear Whoever, I don't want to care for you
Don't want to hold and caress you during any moment
Of weakness you may suffer don't assume
My heart will sympathize.
Love, in me you will find no lies
I don't care for you.

Broken song of wanting
Seven days a week and, Baby, I wont give you one.
My time belongs to me and I prefer
      To spend every waking second alone
I don't want sex or passion
Drugs or alcohol may help my seclusion scheme
Then, again, being under the influence…
      May tear me apart.

Darkness, silence, solitude,
Fuck you, my Love. Leave me to die alone.
You never heard my heart but embraced my attitude.
Now, leave me be.
      Please, let me bear the cold
      On my own.

Part Four

I wish I could tell you, my brother, that all evil
Fades away leaving only strength of heart.
I wish I could tell you, my brother, that all the pain
Ends so graciously as soon as it starts.
But I can't.

My life was abuse and burden, same as yours, brother.
We never asked to be here and now that we're here
Those that brought us here

Forsake us.

You and I, we only find peace in our dreams
Only find hope when no one we know can touch us.
Brother, that same demon beat me till I screamed.
He stomped my face till my mouth bled
Kicked my ribs 'til I felt dead.

Yes, this is it. What we have to look forward to!
Sore arms, torn neck, swollen ribs, slavery and
            Black & blues.
The pain will decide our fate.
The broken heart will question my life.
And if there, with first sight of us, that hate.
My brother, you fight…
You fight to be better then the man
            Oppressing you.

Though, I've never met you brother
I tell you fight. I tell you struggle.
I tell you it's better to die
Knowing you went down like a dragon
And not a victim.

Part Five

And I took hold your arm and held it over the fire,
And it spoke to you, this pain born of a liar,

9

And "Rage is your gift!" it said,

       This violence in your head,

And "Kill till everyone and thing is dead."

And "Touch them all with nitro born of lead."

And "Don't sleep Child.

       Don't stop till you know your hunger."

And it was this demon sat upon your shoulder,

And it took you to your minds most uncharted borders.

And then you were risen of death,

And the sad nonexistence of your life is what you left,

And there she was, angel from the stars,

And the scars…the scars ate your heart,

And so you followed her in your car,

And you drank each of her movements with relish,

And the fire spread, your body it nourished,

And this wrath… it flourished.

And when it was over and she lay broken before you,

And as she died you smiled: "How one became two!"

And you thought of how many more awaited

       Your coming,

And you thought of how you'd begin

       Your spree of killing,

And then it was so…you'd already begun your quest,

And nothing here or there would bring

       Your desire to rest,

And the dragon was born of the fire test,

And in your heart you knew of the past…

       There was nothing left.

Drug Run

I was running to clear my mind
Pavement beneath my feet
Cold air filling my lungs; O, the burn.
The sky was cloudless and though dark
The stars and moon kept the trail visible
I ran to find my soul through fatigue.

Across my path, up ahead in the darkness
Stood three figures lurking, flames in their mouths.
I prepared myself for war tired from my run
Then: Marijuana filled my lungs and I understood.
Revitalized, I understood that they were running, too.
Not with their legs but their lungs and unlike me
       It wasn't towards life but death.

Foreplay

Oh, my love, there's hunger within my unsatisfied heart.
Each day it gets stronger and I fall further away from my
start.
You lay there in front of me, love. Body so enticing, so
beckoning.
My stomach quivers, nerves falter and all I want is us
fucking.

Yes, you read right, my dear sweet passion. Don't play
coy.
Visions of me lickin' your ass, your tits, O, you're my
toy.
I'd push my tongue into you; taste and smell you, so
moist.
I'd fuck you with my mouth, my lips. You'd melt into me
like ice.

And this would be day one. U & I. Tasting, using only
mouths.
We'd kiss and kiss and kiss until one of us lost the bout.
And yes, my love, it'd be how it was when we first began
When childish words were said and you called me your
'Man'.

Put It Away

I bought a card for you on Mother's Day, Mom.
When I got home I wrote how much I love you in it.
      Then I put it in my dresser drawer
          With the other ones.

On your birthday I wanted to mail you a card
But, how could I do that when Dad opens your mail?
      So I put it in my dresser drawer
          And washed away my worry with vodka.

On Valentine's Day I wanted to send you flowers
Could you imagine Dad seeing flowers delivered to you?
      He would have trashed them and then you.
          So I bought and promptly tossed them.

When I turned 28 I wanted you to hold me.
A single hug, a kiss on the brow, something to say you
care
      I wrote this desire in a card and put it away
          Then 40 ounces of beer put me away.

During the birth of my daughter I thought of you
I would have given my arms to have had you beside me
      But, you weren't there… you weren't there,
Mother.

They tell me I think to much, Mom. My hair is white.
They say the past is gone and tomorrow is here

      On New Years day I'll look into the stars, lift my
glass

           And say: "Here's to you, Mom. I still love
you."

Seekers

A group of youths tried to verbally attack my aunt
They thought her alone and elderly, weak and frail.
Stupid actions and youthful ignorance played this stunt.
One physical touch upon her that night and I'd have gone
to jail.

Youth craves fear in others. Youth pushes the boundaries.
When respect should be given they know only wrath and
lust.
But I will not abide by their relentless savageries.
I will not… I refuse to stand there like some puppy lost.

I spoke out, quickly. Rage in my face. Wrath in my heart.
Satan raised me, nurtured me, showed me to crush life.
And though I may have found God animosity towards me
          ends as it begins.
Harsh words will only give the speaker a dose of strife.

There's untold amounts of physical hunger latent within
me.
O, how I dream for a physical opposition to arise
I'd devour and shit out the entirety of my enemies.
I'd hunt down and destroy their blood, become a reaper of
lives.

But this night, the youth resigned confrontation
Perhaps seeing in my eyes the same hunger they dream
of.
I decided to remain silent, to forget my aggression.
So lucky for them my wife taught me how to love.

Lament

Kiss me you stranger
Hold me forever and ever
Only you can make me better
Only you can quench my desire.

Fungus

Fungus on my wall
Growing on my toothbrush.
I woke the other night
Didn't care that I was in hell
Took the fungus from my eyes
Spat it from my loins
And showered away
The plague in my pores.

I washed and washed
But found confliction
When I realized
There was fungus
In my heart.

Late

It's so late
My eyes burn
Stomach is churning
Moon is shining
Family sleeping.
When will it be my turn?
A calm hand at fate
Soul all yearning
But I'm up tryin' to learn.
In this I'm built of faith.
      Can't stop learning.
      Can't stop fighting.
Weak as hell when I was born
When I was born I was full of hate
Out my window I can see the moon
It's watching me.
Fatigue should be here soon
Then I'll sleep.

America Allowed

America turned me into a prostitute
The TV told me to sell my ass to be rich
Philip Morris gave me a cigarette and took my lungs
McDonald's gave me a burger and took my stomach

America allowed this; took my money

Johnny Walker gave me a pint and took my liver
Nike gave me some shoes and took my feet
Apple gave me an Ipod and took my ears
Colgate gave me fluoride and took my mouth

America allowed this; took my money

Bill Gates gave me a CPU and took my brain
Sony gave me a Playstation and took my eyes
Democracy gave me freedom and took my heart
Society gave me a standard and fucked me 'til I bled

America allowed this; took my money

Now I look at what I have
Now I think about what I had
I have to get my daughter away from TV
I have to get her out of America.

"America, you can't have her; take me instead!"

and America said: "Hahaha, why? You're already dead."

Those Before

Oscar was imprisoned for being homosexual
Fyodor was imprisoned for reading a letter
Ernest couldn't take it anymore so he ended it all
So did that great 'Bell Jar', Sylvia.

Walt needed a shave and some hair dye
Cumming's needed some hair, period.
Yeats? Yeats? What'd he say, again?
Allen? Now, that was a Beat gifted with pen.

Everybody wanted and wants to be Edgar
Dead in some gutter, smile on face, riddled liver.
In the aisle the other day, the aisle of B&N
Page after page and none but Maya bore the title
        Poet.

Until I found the poetry section
Running my fingers across hundreds of spines
I died in front of that wall of multitudes
My back facing the fiction and my heart…
        My heart kissing the feet of those mentioned
        Above.

I, Cold

Cold night it is
      Bone chilling.
'I' is cold
'V' is cold
      but me…
In this frigid _____
      I feel safe.

Disappointment

Reign of the shit king
High on his throne of bling-bling
He called me over one night
The shit king said:
>"Poet, tell me of a great tragedy."
I knelt and slow approached the blight.
Hesitant, I carefully replied:
>"O, great king, what would you know of me?"

Sleep

You don't want to sleep
       I can't force dreams upon you
Myself? Where is life?
       Let alone dreams,
           Let alone dreams.

Once I fell in love with that scape
       Murk covered dreamscape.
Pissed myself and mattress that night
       Shit filled memory quilt.

O, innocence and purity
       Of its filth, eat it right
Off a plate of pure fetus feces
       Smile, lap your lips and burp.

With dreams like these, my love
       I ask: "You don't want to sleep?"
And understand any reply you should
       Wish; pray to wake in the morning.

But fret not, little one with the curls
       No daemon, dragon, devil, sleeps beneath you.
Aaaggrrhh, beside you, I smile at this,
       You will always find me, body a shield

Ready to brake you free of any
Nightmare!

Spoon

Nonina* of the stars
       Forming in your hands meatballs.
Mixing the tomato sauce with that part-time spoon.
Part-time mixer = Part-time weapon
       Disciplinary. Nonina, that spoon
       In your hand…
              We trembled.

From the morning till sunset
       That spoon made the best food, the best food.
From sunset 'til sunrise
That spoon fixed whatever error we made
       Our asses bright red
       Juicy like the tomato sauce
           Swollen.

I think of then, Nonina
How I've dreamed of returning to then…
       With you…
       And yes…
           that spoon.

* Nonina is Grandma in Italian.

Free, Now

Who are you?
Walk into my world an unknown.
I saw someone like you once
Laying dead in the suds of an
       Empty beer can.
Yeah, you were blond, then (off blond).

O you brought out that evil-evil
In me; my heart hurt so much then.
But, here you are, again.
Though your flesh reeks of difference
There's… there's familiarity.
       A cold breeze across my cheeks
       Fire, HELL, on my lips.

Love, whoever you are,
I don't want to know you then
Or ever; how I wish time were ignorant.
Flesh has no longer. That mystery
Uumm, desire once was but has no reign
Here in my now, in my waking rebirth.

Pass me the shears, Stranger.
Are they sharp? Do they implode morality?
Kneel over a moment, yes, rest your head

In my lap while I pretend to care.
Close your eyes, dear. SNIPSNIPSNIP!
No more hair. Yes, love, were free, now.

Riddance

E hated her abusing-adulterous husband
"Oh, but he's a good provider." She'd lie.
Eyes blood shot. Hair thinning. There could be
      No lie.

Day in and day out, during our hours
Of sharing our melancholic association
She'd confess the horrors of lovers
"…they call him all the time." Ran her confession.

As time would move, hungry for its course
E left our humble occupation for _____.
Such things are inevitable; finality.
Life is but a way station amidst a tsunami.

I had the opportunity to see E once more
Months and months later. I had forgotten her true face.
"Hi, Joe!" she smiled, lovely almond shaped eyes.
Full head of hair. There could be
      No lie.

When I asked: "What's your secret, E?
How is it you look so young, look so young?"
She said: "Oh, dear sweet Joe. Didn't you hear?
A month ago my husband died in a freak accident."

She hugged me and I truthfully accepted.

Neighbor

(I'm waiting for that woman to die.
Death has got to be here for her soon.
She looks like death
She smells like death
Talks like death
       Wait… maybe, she's death.)

Eyes all body searchin' my soul
Spotted hag hands all reachin' for my loins
Treacherous demon tongue pressed into my ear
I wanna kill your face, it's hypnotizing
Chop those fuckin' hands off
Those feet… poison steps.

Hidin' behind your brick and glass
All a buzz about the world outside your door
I wanna kill your mouth, Death. It's
Useless bullshit placed there like some cruel joke
She said: "Hello!" to me the other day, smiled and smiled.
I gave one back and said: "Fuck you, Grotesque."

(Next door neighbor!)
I was shitting the other night when she interrupted:
"Must you be so noisy?" she asked, purple bags for eyes,
       Garlic for a tongue.

I didn't answer, just closed the door, returned to the toilet.
And said aloud: "Oh, look, a portrait of my next door
Neighbor. Smells like her, too!"

Glimpse

For my little brother, William, who wasn't given life.

They say your name would have been William.
I can see you now in my minds eye smoking.
During the rain storm, brother, we'd drink.
Share the bottle like brothers should, no difference.
We'd talk of girls and woman, share our secrets.
Oh, how we'd sit together and laugh conquests.

I'd tell you my dreams and make you apart of them
I'd expect you to undoubtedly do the same, no questions.
(How would we come home after a night at the stadium?)
When dragons wanted to war with me, you'd stand along
side me.
Broken leg: you carried me home. Broken soul: you
carried me…
Brother, though we've never met, I miss you.

Ramble

Practice makes perfect and this is what I must practice in
Order to secure a great and powerful standing in this
Graciously unforgiving wretched country I was so happily
Raised in by my father, Hatred, during the 80/90's when
I thought writing was the greatest art in all the
Fucking galaxies (except Xibalba) put together into
A massive condom on my dickhead before penetration
Could be accomplished practice had to be practiced
because
One slip… just one slip and a galaxy could swim
Free and if that Goddamned shit should spontaneously
Happen pick up a gun and shoot your face off now
While you still have a choice in the matter otherwise
Stick it out day by day and hope with a little
Milk and practice you might become a poet.

Alex

For my cousin

The ignorance of youth!
O how it reeks of beauty, of passion.
Youth is forgiveness and grudge
It's desire and rage... rancid rage.
How can the relics of past ever judge
Those creatures of light coming of age?
Youth compliments and insults
Has sarcasm branded into its sinew.

Alex has a drink!
His defiance and hunger... purity.
Drink after drink, smile cousin,
How beautiful you are.
Even God saw it, you, that moment
I saw you, looking not at the universe
But yourself
So concerned for your flesh.

On the floor swimming through realms
Alcohol having its way with your weakness (ignorance)
Even then, my cousin, you were beauty
Comprised of innocence (Drink!)
For it's when we love reality, locked to it
That we forget how luscious life can be.

I say drink, young Alex

For tomorrow… tomorrow we make love

  To true tragedy: living.

The Guide

Man stands
Defiant and strong.
Thinks of nothing but himself
Loves only the image of himself.
Stranger I don't know
Weakened with addiction
I was once something great
I fucked!
Yes, I fucked… and I was good.
And I loved… yes, I loved.

He came to me stranger in knowledge
He asked me for help standing defiant.
"My path? I wish to follow you." He said.
I kissed his hand and said:
"No, my brother, we will both, side by side,
Set the example." Because I am unity.
We held hands a moment, brothers.
And when he was ready, ready to be
I stepped away from him, found strong drink
Looked high and shouted to the heavens,
　　　　To the stranger:
"Keep going, Brother! I await the others.
For I must show them what I've shown you."

He called me liar
And as I sipped my poison
I thought him right.

Victoria

Victoria of the fire
Born of flame with envy
They gave you life, left you dreams
Forced you to be a woman and murdered
Your childhood was lost long before
      It was born.

But, Victoria, last of a dead species,
You gave breath to a newer stronger lineage.
St. Concrete I shall call you.
For you were victorious when the street
Was your home. You were a lioness
And a dove when you had to be.
      So, for you, my Victoria, a kiss
      Because you brought end to our weakness.

Eight

Eight rounds fired into the air
Eight rounds a new year is here.
Eight rounds one hit some kid
Eight rounds lounged itself right in his head.
Eight rounds should have been shot into the ground.
      Instead, a life won't see a new year
            Because one round struck him down.

Charmer

He thought himself snake resistant
Picked it up and manhandled it.
"Snake Charmer!" he declared.
Seconds later he was bitten dead.

Bonfire

The flames of the bonfire and we sat around it
Born of different mothers but brothers in life.

Smoke filled our clothing, blackened the sky
And we talked of how we were supposed to be.
"We lost." I said, no disagreement in any gaze.
My two words had summed up our lives, our hells.

Give me a chance to show you out
Man, brother, we'll stand together in this.
Break this shit existence we're so stuck in.
Like flames… reaching for the dark heavens.

"Why have we lost?" Savage asks, sadness in his eyes
Answers and truth, acceptance and pain
Pain of nerves being touched with greed.
How could I answer him? I, being simply, man.

There was silence
It was what it should have been.
That night…
We watched the smoke, our dreams.

The flames of the bonfire and we sat around it
Born of different mothers but brothers in death.

Singing

You were singing, my little love
Tears and my eyes were swollen.
You were singing, my little love
And all evil in me was broken.

So happy and joyous was I
Listening to your precious voice
O how I was once a putrid lie
Now your existence has left bliss
       My only choice.

Making up the rhythm as you went along
Throwing in words here and there; one and two
Father and daughter our bond will remain strong
And, little one, as you sang, all my dreams
       Became dreams of you.

My Love

It's your calling, your promise
That has made this day this day.
Choice etched into your left
Destiny branded into your right
It doesn't matter if you're not the best
Just as long as you put up a fight.

Study and train
Practice through pain
I'm tired already
I can't be this forever
Look out into the gloom
And know it's true
That I'm not the only one
Not that tortured soul
Standing alone.

Leave

I don't want to know who you are.
Don't want to know where you're from.
Like fresh NY Broadway star
Just let me know when you're gone.

Born of Me

For Isis Margaret Padron

I'm sorry, my love, for you were born of me.
You got dealt a bad hand with me as your dad.
Poverty devoured my soul long before your birth
And my body… my body belongs to alcohol.

No one can say I didn't try, my baby,
I gave it my all and so much more.
Words that made angels cry fell from my hands.
Fourteen hour days I worked and fought.

When the world felt too heavy
Your mother tried to carry me.
Alas, my burden broke her strength
And holding hands we fell into nothing.

My collar up I face the cold forever
With you beside me, my love, and though
I may be your burden, Isis Margaret
You're the only reason I keep fighting:

The string holding together whatever
Hope remains in me.

The Kitchen of P.S. 204

Almost ten years I've worked
Broke my back in this place.

Making sandwiches when the Towers fell
Watched Bush kill thousands.

Right here, I saw it all.
I haven't a penny to my name

My pockets have long forgotten cash.
In November... O how I wanted to leave

But, now, Gerald Ford died
While I was making sandwiches

Cookin' ravioli with Saddam hangin'
Maybe Hilary (the smart Clinton)
        Will make life better.

I'll make 62,400 hamburgers
During her four years in the house

Sandwiches, sandwiches, politics, United Nations
We both have immense work ahead of us.

Rats

There's a rat in the crops
Watching, waiting, striking.
There's a rat in my crop
Laughing, smiling, informing.

I know who you are standing there beside me
Listening to my every word, showing concern
My sweet-sweet enemy, I know you're there
Plotting and planning to see me burned.

Set by broken chance, by stolen choice
You won't stop my dance. You won't silence my voice
Foreknowledge of who you are has stayed the blade
And so, with strength and will, I hold fast
      The legacy I have made.

Plans

I have loved you
Though I've never been true
Child, in me you will learn devotion
You will become a great abuser of emotion
And together, parent and kin
We will abandon our roads of sin.

Family O' Mine

We fell apart
Broken parts
Of a whole
Lost soul
Searching for
An open door
To the stars
Our lives
Behind bars.

I won't forget
Dad and his bet
Mom, I miss you
And your Nike shoes
So much anger
Turned me 'stranger'
Born of depreciation
How we fucked insane.

Grandma in the sky
I cried when you died
Laying in your coffin
We felt something
So cruel,
Wrath our tools

Nonina, mistress of hate
How I was your saint.

Margaret up above
Built of so much love
Smiling that smile
Bearing the wild
You bought calm
Sang us psalms
Of forgiveness
Stripped us of madness.

Uncle who stole
More then my soul
Soiled bitch
Lost in a ditch
I'd give you a kiss
But you live with shit
Such is such
Man, I hate you so much.

And Aunt Vickie
Holding down sanity
Tryin' to form a family
Tryin' to love through tragedy
You're the head blood
The new mother of our brood
We'll love you forever

Your being our treasure.

And how of misshapen
Family of love broken
Has now and tomorrow
Tasted sorrow
Will we ever be free
Of our tsunami sea?
Blessed family, what I can tell
Is in the end we're all going
            To Hell.

Amore

We worked out last night under the stars
Masturbation on a mattress soaked in sweat
Screaming people in the night lights forever
Burning holes into the sight of ass and cock
They loved it they said they loved it
I have forgotten the glory of procrastination
Hear me! I've forgotten
Vero said it got bigger
Outside of our open window, into a clear
Night, there in the sky, a moon as
Big as my ass
We fell in love with it
We wanted more then we could give
But saw in our flesh dreams and orgasm
Moist fluids pouring off sinew
Into my mouth, onto my loins, my balls
Vero asked if I liked it
I told her to kiss my tongue
She did. We lived. We shared. We died.
We fucked, brought tears, shit blood.
Someone screaming in the pitch
Someone lost
I love you, whoever you are.

Credentials

I lost whatever footing I had on life with my birth
And the darkness, and the light, and the pain, the thirst.
You were given this moment at first, a moment like no
other
To learn just one simple truth: You were born to suffer.

That burning light at the edge of mother
That eternal question: "Where's my father?"
Pushing through the flesh, the hair, the screams
The death of expectations, you've seen this once before
It hid with the thumping beat of mother's heart
Invaded my little body, filled my stomach with dreams.

Who were we before this beginning, you and me?
That crevice of which we lived broken, sodden, forsaken
Never changed, never once spoke of unknown, of
knowledge
Tears weren't. Love couldn't. And at our most purist of
form
Form untarnished, did we care?
The gate we arrive through dies upon our awakening.
Heartbeats drown in torment, in fatigue.

And this, my love, is our new existence:
In that face you hold lies one single fact

In order to lose you must first have
In order to have you cannot be
And in order to be you must know loss.

My Little Love

For Isis

There's a feeling I get when I look at you
Call it love… but love is just a word
Trying to touch at something it hasn't a clue of.

You could say it's your curly hair
Someone could claim it to be your puggish nose
But I know what it is I see there hidden
Within those giant almond shaped eyes of yours.

Me! My little love, I see me.
And, yes, with each passing day I'm reassured
Of your life baring such a meaning as to not be explained
There when you rescued me from myself, in my dreams
I was so certain of it
When you kissed me goodnight it was there
Pushing into my chest, breaking through flesh and bone
Undeterred.

For you, my little love
I have come to one torpid conclusion:
No matter your path, no matter my addiction
Simply falter but a step and I shall be there to catch you.
I shall pave your way
I shall push aside all obstacles

I shall suffer all sacrifices for you.

And if you should want to know who I am
This man that has declared his life for you.
I can answer you with such great pride:
I am your hope, your faith and fear, your father.

Dwell

Demons in your minds eye break bread with reality
Twisting conception, blurring truth with fantasy
Actions you never made get played over and over
In your head with questions you've asked so many times
before.

I don't care for the wrongs I've done
Nor the promises I've so viciously broken
I was born a ball of phlegm in Gods throat
Hands blessed with infection, this'll have to be
      My attempt at a suicide note.

Those horrors in times mouth, twisting, refusing to die
Eating away at your soul like alcohol on putrid flesh
FUCK tattooed on my forehead: a reference to that
time…
It doesn't matter. Never did… our crimes, our lies.

Seated on my toilet pushing, aiming, praying.
Demons corrupting my hands, loving my burdens.
I've finally made way for the gift of crying
For the hope that maybe tomorrow won't end so lovingly
      Broken.

Patience

For Margaret Padron

Beep... Beep... Beep...
The nurse said she had just fallen to sleep
Amidst the torturous sounds of machinery fighting
For her life meant needles and swollen legs
I took that seat beside her bed, looked at the untouched
Tray of tasteless food on her bed table.
Oprah was on her TV talking in silence.
Beep... Beep... Beep... and the sun rested on her
        Uncovered feet.

There was a time, I see you now, smiling
Walking that pigeon walk of yours, always
Concerned for this broken nephew of yours.
I was your little liar.
I always told you I was fine.
Shattered face at your door at three in the a.m.
Blood filled mouth; it was the first time I asked
For your help, the first time I found myself alone
In this world where pain is always on sale.

No hesitation that night and I was so thankful
No starry sky or frozen clouds or bashed in stomach.
Just her acceptance and the pain didn't matter.
Eyes open you looked at me, so weak, the table turned

My burden called father yours called cancer.

With hug and kiss I run my fingers through her hair.
"How long have you been here?" she asks. I see it's been
Over an hour and answer: "Only about four or five
minutes."
"You're the only one that never wakes me up." She
smiles,
Taking my hand in hers and wasting the little strength
She had left.

In my heart that day I answered her with: "I once woke
you
In the a.m. hours. And like the angel you are you saved
me
That night and forever."

My Muse

You,
My sweet love,
Angel with golden wings,
Hair of halo bliss.

You,
My sweet love,
Of stars born in pitch,
Suns lit by lips.

I've held you in my dreams
Kissed you in my suffering.
My sweet love,
I've loved you with reams of pulp.

Brothers

We gave up long-long ago, my lost friend.
Where the mornings found us as brothers
Afraid of nothing but time
Drunk with the knowledge of a full days work
        Before us.

When the oven would ring and the pastries would shine
golden
The wake of morning followed our progress, our sacrifice.
Then the others would come and we, shepherds to the
late,
Would guide them the rest of the way
        To what it meant to earn every dollar,
        From the moon to the sun and back to the moon.

Fourteen,
Sixteen hour days,
We were brothers through time, family built by reliance.
I loved you, my friend, then and now.
Though I may never know you again
        Please hear me when I say:
        "Born with the blood of Judas
        I gave life to our final story.
        And, my brother, when I see us
        All I want to say is I'm sorry."

Anger

My flesh burns
With this broke down rage.
I have no sense to stop it.
Sacrifice my tortured mind,
Patience ate time,
Love so undefined,
Burn me,
Broke down rage.

And you loved me my enemy!

You're always there
In my veins,
Always in my face
Leave this place, leave me.
I've lost my dreams making love to you.
I've lost so much life making love with you.

Give me a third chance.
I want another time
Another life
Another crime.
Let me roll up into a ball
And roll away.

Exercise

Sit-ups to quench the sounds.
3000 and the enemy losses his voice.
Push-ups to brake the face.
3000 and the enemy bleeds sympathy.

"Faggot!" he screams. "Fucking-useless-faggot!"
3000 dips and you'll be alright.
Those words, the ones that punctured your chest,
Exploded your lungs and imploded your belly,
They were formed with nothing but good intention.

"Bitch!" he screams. "Fucking-bitch-faggot!"
3000 pull-ups and he's almost gone.
Your body takes the pain
And your mind forgets everything but:
2998…
2999…
3000!

Convicts exercise with great amounts of determination
Calling it an enthusiastic desire to survive.
With only their cell they use physical improvement
To ensure survival.

"Bitch!" he screams. "Faggot!"
I was eleven.
My twin sized bunk bed
Fought every count with me.

The Bronx

The Bronx and it's one of those cold winters
Nights a mixture of clouds and clarity.
A little beer in the system and its only clarity.

You're a creature of the night and the night ain't endin'
tonight.
You're a New Yorker in the frigid Bronx dressed for sex
and drugs.
You're a few shots too drunk and it should be this way
every day.

Dance-dance-dance your troubles away sweet lover of the
Bronx.
Pill here! Pill there! And wherever you were two minutes
ago...
Yeah, you came to the party dressed for success, for
desire.
Yeah, you came to the party suffering from that fuckin'
fire.

At that next physical,
After the Doctor confesses your inevitable premature
death
You'll say:
        "Hey, Doc, I live in the Bronx!

You could die takin' a shit…
If you know what I mean."
And the Doc:
"You're absolutely right.
What type of insurance do you have again?"

We Fall

We fall is all
We tryin' to be somethin' were not
It's our story
Our passion.
Take your gifts you lost pain…
Away with you!
There's the door.
'cause whether it's yes
Or no
When it comes to us
God doesn't even know.

Hunger

And the flesh is the cause of this hunger,
The flesh and its hunger for more then it is.
Your eyes covet and then your soul is corrupted.
Your hands touch and then your loins burst
       Vomit is your sense of acknowledgement.
       Shit is your final judgment.

Trials

We fought our fate… you and me.
We lived our love and loved so free.
But then there's life and wretched streams
Born of lust, addicted to poison dreams.

A decade and we forgot our fate
Remembrance always comes so late.
Through the trials… which were tumultuous
My own desire took precedence.

We could pave a new path, my love
Try to fix the feeling we were once built of…
And if this doesn't work for we two
My love, know that I never wanted
      To hurt you.

My Name Is Help

I got this holy trinity inside my
Refrigerator I have freedom in cans.
Show and give some green paper
Pow! Just like that you're a member.
High society.

At the meeting's you know it's there
Hiding inside your fellow members:
"Hello, my name is Help. I'm an alcoholic."
But they can't hear me.
I don't talk loud enough.

Praying to the holy trinity
My three intoxicating cans of
Drunken enlightenment;
My all I ever wanted from life
I begin to understand my existence.

Fosters, Heineken, and Bud light,
Coors the sweet creature,
Guinness and the anger is dead,
Beck's and God lives in my head.
Oh, my love, my Corona.

Modelo and the itch is silent.
Old English and I'm thinkin': "What twitch?"
St. Ides and I love this poison ride.
"Hello, my name is Help. I'm an alcoholic."
And this started way back when I wished
      Dad had let me die,
      Back when I had reason to run.

40

40 ounces and your job is gone.

40 ounces and your death is born.

40 ounces and some innocent is D.O.A.; Hit and run.

40 ounces and your kid dreads today: You're washed up; done.

40 ounces with a back to back sentence.

40 ounces and God withholds his presence.

40 ounces and the dog shits by the door.

      No way out… feces all over the floor.

40 ounces and you forget to say you're sorry.

40 ounces love is some sad story.

40 ounces and I shot my foot off.

40 ounces and I leapt from my loft.

40 ounces and Satan said: "Hi!"

40 ounces and "Oh, Shit! I died."

Clammy

That bastard is on his way
I saw him in the toy store today.
Smelling me,
Wrapping his clammy fingers
Around my neck.

"I love you." He whispers into my ear.
Every time that minute hand moves
His fingers gain strength.
Every time that heart of mine beats
That bastard gives me a little more hate.

There's a grave somewhere,
And I feel it every time I forget how
        To care.

Reunite

Bring me love from somewhere…somewhere…
Leave me songs of how precious you were.
Oh, I remember how it was when you were here
How much you adored me! How you killed my fear.

Two more eternities, my lost one.
Just mere moments and yes, we'll meet again.
Like the striking strength, bond, of mother and son
We'll be together once more, when it's over,
        When the last song has been sung.

Lost

Where?
Where the stars shine
Drunk, my brother, on wine.
Thinking of where… a year from now.
Thinking of just how
I'll get there.

Answer?
It wasn't in the bottle
But answers never breed in bottles
Nothing comes from bottles.
>   *When I'm sure of this*
>   *I'll know which star*
>   *To place my wish.*

Confusion

I found God in a can of Fosters.
Right there on my bed, imported lager in hand
25.4 fluid ounces down the old pipe
And I swear to God it was God himself
        Laying beside me.

He looked a lot like my wife.
"What you doin', God?" I asked.
"Lesson plan's for work on Monday." God answered.
"God?" I asked.
"You're drunk!"
"No!"
"Don't lie."
"Uuuugghh… a little." I confessed.

Sleep began to creep up on me and exhaustion
Still staring at God I said: "Good night, God."
And she answered: "Good night, honey.
Too bad you're drunk you were going to get
        Lucky tonight."

But I did get lucky.
The night was a success.
I had my favorite beer.
I met God and found out he looked like my wife.

And I got some rest.
God always waits for me to get drunk
      Before confusing me!

Eyes of Light

The lights that come from your eyes
Remind me of how much it meant
For us to accept that life we choose
To share so rigorously together.

There were pictures I once saw
Of a nebula with spider-leg blue flames
And blood red dust clouds.
Oh, when I look at the light
That bleeds from your eyes
   I know desire.

Long Have I Looked

Long Have I looked for the road to freedom
And found only the cold hardships of addiction.
Drink has corrupted my mind and polluted my body
Smoke has filled my awareness with abscess.
Sex has given me lust, broken desire
And none has given to me the luxury of trust,
      They deem me the anonymous liar.

Ah, but freedom was never guaranteed.
It doesn't have bonds or emotions
Freedom isn't addiction or acceptance.
Long have I wanted to explain freedom
To shed light to all of its beauty.
But such a task would truly be futile
      For I've never known it's
      touch.

Omega

Something in me tells me who I am
How I am is a crushed piece of pulp
Plastered against a molten wall of shit.

Lost stapled me to the crime some time
Ago I lost all my hope with a kiss not
Worth three pennies and a nickel.

Pride and I left my fathers web
To face a world of fuck-u-over
So childishly unprepared and all that.

Two: they stand there in my shadow
Persecuting me, blinding me, releasing
Me into a world of unsatisfied dreams.

Yes, and dreams are never seen
Or fulfilled, cold and treacherous,
Long and hard all ways through it.

But I'm comprised of the two
As I am star born of shit sinew
Lighting the way for thousands.

My giant head of deadly sin

Shall be the omega of my line
Omega and something in me dies.

Omega and my dreams become legend
Omega and my dick triples in size
Omega and marijuana opened my eyes
Omega, fuck you! Omega touched me
        And now I know the song
Omega and my blood needs filterin'
Much as much can ever be
Omega and my soul is set free.

On pulp or modern shit
Sprinkled with lust or buried in pride
No sex and I'll die from the disease
No dreams and I'm now and forever American
        (That's what the TV said.)
        (Trust me!)

I have gone omega
My view of omega has gone omega
Grandfather Chaos before me
        Went omega
Father Gluttony (I came from his balls)
        He has gone omega
My unborn son (born of pride and lust balls)
        He, Greed, shall go omega.

There's no stopping the endless

Cycle the passion of working for bills

Omega bills! Omega the landlord! Omega taxes!

And all generations shall know, there is

An everyday suffering…

      It's called living.

Loyalty

Drunken bastard stomped his dog
Kicked him, spat him, cursed him.
Dog yelped, screaming in dog language
       --Help!

With closed fist I approached the
Drunken bastard with means of war
Fury in my heart and death in my eyes.

"Touch that dog, again!" I dared.
"Fuck-off." He mumbled.
"Touch that dog, again, and I'll
       Show you Satan.

He raised his hand to strike the dog
The dog cowered, broken by man
Shattered and suicidal with grief.

I went to stop the bastard
Prepared to shove my fist through his head
When the dog leapt up and attacked me,
       Bit me.

Next time:
With a smile on my face (a big smile)

I'll let that mutha-fucka get beat to death.

Concrete

While walking to work I dissolved
       Into the concrete.
Having had walked the path times numerous
God said: "Thus, you become one
       With the concrete."

I didn't cry. Destiny torn to pieces
Then God said: "Fret not, Child.
       For the pavement you are now
       One with shall teach millions
       More of what you were."

Now, built of cold stone, I cried.
He asked why such an act
       Knowing full well my heart.
       "My path was a path of hopelessness."

And he answered: "Aaarrgghh, but your soul,
       Your soul made me so proud."
Time dried my tears…
And I accepted.

Drink

There's an agony
On my liver.
Sweet tragedy
Is called Budweiser.

Can after can
I fall into vanity.
Working this putrid land
I've forsaken sanity.

Just a moments rest
I plead with the drink.
But now it's in my chest
Now it's all I think.

Whatever test: I failed
I'm an alcoholic.
Let lessons be told
My life was somethin'
       Tragic.

Prostitute

O young prostitute of the flesh
Selling your soul for so much less.
Do you know the price you'll pay
For giving your body away?

I can't tell you the world will forgive
I can't give you a pure reason to live
But what I know, young child
Is the sadness of your flesh gone wild.

No, I will not pay you
Nor think of touching you.
Young prostitute of the flesh
With true love I wish you the best.

Try to fight back
Resist the pull of the trick.
His power is in cash.
Such power ends fast.

Fight that pimp boss
Pot O' Boilin' water and no loss
Kiss him / her goodbye
And give life…
        Give life another try.

Bus

Patience today
Got to have it when lateness hurts
Things go wrong and, man, I feel
      Like I'm goin' to burst.

Got to breath
Got to calm my speed
Anxiety and, yes,
I want beer.

Vero said I'm going to die in a rush
Dead with the lights (blinding)
Head hurts but wait…
There it is.
My bus.
I feel better, now.

Words

O words of falsehood
Tormenting the innocent
No words of brotherhood
I suffer this madness.

They spit opinions on me
Look for my stand on it all.
Fuck this mad treachery
Show me the nearest door.

Run away with my head high
Cut my ears off,
        Leave 'em behind
Kiss my ass goodbye
I want nothin' to do with
        Your bind.

Expectations

There's something wretchedly painful
       Catching up to me, waiting for me.
Walking to work, the sun still hidden
       I can feel it coming, touching.

My head hurts with this knowledge
       Maybe I've adopted to well a routine?
Yes, it could be I fear change, but…
       Something in that pitch wants me
       To rearrange. (My life.)

But I can't end who I am
       Just up and quit, make that sacrifice.
I found a copy of Abstraction in B&N
       Last night and last night I was
       Proud to be who I am.

No Sleep

That creature sleep eludes me
Steps further away every night

(No sleep and dreams cannot be
No sleep and I'm too tired to fight.)

Vero tells me I need rest
Tells me I'm too nervous.

God knows I've tried my best
My dreams have become scarce.

Maybe strong drink could help
But, God, I feel like dying.

Trapped in this Hell… in this Hell.
I can't keep reality from lying.

And Sex

And sex is the cure to all illness
Sex and that cancer is no more
As if it never were
Passion and fucking your inner core
Tied to a bed of nails
Blind face buried in a pussy
Darkness was all I knew
And now, now I can see.
It doesn't matter the physical
Illness, virus, devouring your flesh & soul
Sex
Sex
And more sex
Let pain be forgotten and lust be told
Let genitals and mouths become one
Single fucked soaked lover
Sweet love, when they ask you why?
Tell them you've forgotten how to
Suffer.

Irritation

Irritation all over my face.
I want to scratch.
Take sand-paper and scrub.

But, that's how this all started.

I touched something
Then: I touched my face.
Now: I irritate.

Such patience not to indulge.

Remember

Can we remember who we are?
Can we see the horizon, the stars?
Does it at all matter, the song of a fall?
The great suffering of a waking dream?

3

You gave me three reasons
To shoot myself in the face:
      1. You showed me difference
      2. You taught me choice
      3. And you gave me hope.

An Answer

There was a moment I gave in
While coming home on the bus
I saw the uselessness of it all.
Life?
Why?
And then I knew… love.

Fallen Angel

I stood up and fell down
Looked around felt the ground
Didn't make a sound.

Thought myself dead
Broken face and dehaloed head.
"Take care!" God had said.

But I wasn't lost
Angel came down played host
Told me I was a ghost.

I resisted this pain
Broken reality insane
Stand up, the poet, the reign.

And I never fell, again.
Having had learned from the end
I'd already learned in heaven.
   (Such refusal!)

Mustang

Mustang at 90 mph
Mustang at 190 mph
The world beyond the highway a blur
Seatbelt off at 60 mph

We were going as fast as life hates
We were ageless and sons to no man.

Children of blood shed and speed
Believed in us with longing and need.

Somewhere at 150 mph
We lost our hood.
Somewhere at 160 mph
God no longer understood.

We played this game with a horrible bet
We played, lost life and won death.

Thief

Stolen milk!
Stolen milk!
She didn't have to steal from me.
Thief of milk.
Who is she but my sister?
Why degrade her self in such a way?
Plastic bag open
No hesitation
No preoccupation
I lost you woman.
That milk in your bag…
That would have quenched
      The thirst of some poor
      Dehydrated child.
But now it's in your bag
Losing its usefulness
To your greed.
I will not forgive you, sister.
Those children…
There's one difference
Between you and them:
Their still innocent.

Love Verse

I can say it no other way
This is verse of how much I love you.
My stranger, lover or enemy.
My equal, brother or sister.

Young woman pushing a stroller.
Young child looking out into the world
O mother standing behind, watching,
Caring, loving, smoking.
You are my family
I love you.

O you giant of a man
That scar across your neck
It tells me great suffering.
I don't know you my African brother
But I would have fought those demons
That tried to end your life.
I love you.

Young teen coming from school
Bag full of books; eyes full
Of fatigue. Hard work ahead.
Long nights of study. I'm there
With you reading, writing, learning.

Yours is a never ending journey,
Λ verse of knowledge, teen,
I love you.

O young woman in your chair
Trapped in it forever, until.
Crippled and unable to run
Into the fields with me.
I'll carry you in my arms
Not with sympathy but respect.
I love you and your struggle.

Young attractive woman standing
Relishing in your beauty
You give failing hearts meaning.
And though sex is a powerful inspiration
I don't love you for such a petty concept.
What I love in you, of you,
Is your pride.

Young drug addict, my brother.
I tasted the same hungers you have.
I loved them. I love them still.
I wish you strength on your journey
To the stars. Beside you, in the dark
Matter I shall be.
I love you.

This is verse of how much I love you.
And, yes, my strangers, there will be
A day in which I meet you all
But that day isn't.
Not yet, love. Not yet.

$ Life

For George Smith and the countless souls lost at sea.

O to put a price on a human life.
They were on their honeymoon. Lovers.
Husband & wife.
Star struck and so lost in passion
They shared each other like dreams
They loved each other like orbits.
And the cruise they were on
Was merely a moment of their bond.

Poor George Smith
You'll be missed.
Lost in the great Aegean Sea
Lover, husband, Royal Caribbean tragedy.
One million in the hands of Jennifer
And now your justice is over
For what was looked on as a murder incident
Is now just some lame accident.

Imagine how many millions have been spent
Using this type of justice?

Angst

I made love to my routine today
And now I'm at loss for words.
Sitting here in the dark and gray
Tryin' to find lines that work.

But it's as though poetry eludes me
Of all things that should vanish.
Comin' to terms with my blocked mind sea
My stomach hurts somethin' savage.

I can't take this desire to do somethin'
Much more grandiose then myself.
I can't take the thought of ending
My life with a single book on my shelf.

Lump

There's a lump in my head
Beneath the skin.
I think that soon I'll be dead
Deceased as soon as I began.

Such irony is priceless
Such payment is mandatory.
I tormented many into madness
And now reap the penalties.

I've decided not to go to a doctor.
I'll deal with it how I will
And should my life become a little shorter
I'll leave Vero a little cash for bills.

Omega Lovers

(I am forest of today on paved street
Built of steel, glass, concrete,
Built of flesh, sex, deceit,
The trees are made of blood and veins
The roots: cock, balls, clit, ass.
Its brain blessed with anal pain.
We have for hair pubic grass
Our bark? Sinew cooked till consistency
Has carved into it our great tragedy
The omega of our broken, forever.)

A young woman in our eyes
Gave her flesh to some putrid guy (or guys)
Fucked, sucked, shit on, and passed along
Oh how she loved men handsome and strong.
Disease passed her by and God gave her child
Such a great benefit to your actions in the wild.
Felt the beat of the child's heart within
Born from the actions of lust, that great sin.
But, Love, who's the blessed father?
Or does it not matter, sweet mother?

Alcoholic brother lost on the floor of time
Drinkin' never let you down; drinkin' isn't a crime.
Bottle after bottle, can after can, heaven sent

Drank it all down, every sud, every drop, hell bent
No one in your life mattered then, now, tomorrow.
You have your own vomit filled beautiful sorrow.
I am forest of today on paved drunk streets
Built of rancid flesh, soiled sex, and brewed deceit.
The other night I saw the glory of God in the sky
Tomorrow, my brother, we drink till we die.

And we two must remain together
The omega of our broken, forever
The drunk bastard and the pregnant slut
Driving towards unity on a condom of sanity
Tryin' so damned hard, like dead trees, to end the rut.
But the struggle, the pain, is bordering insanity.
We kissed each other while lost in dreams.
We loved each other till love wasn't what it seemed.
And there was no goodbye, love, for us
Because, with tears, we were born of sloth and lust
        (Broken, forever).

Children

Does it at all matter?
That path we haven't traveled,
The line we dread to cross,
The mysteries we have yet to unravel?

I laughed yesterday
When I heard news of a child's falling.
I laughed yesterday
Because his flight was born Superman acting.

Domestic Dispute

When we take
When we make
It doesn't matter
We're the masters
Of our faith
Of our faith
Born of wings
Dipped in silence
Lovers torn twice
I fuck the violence
Of our faith
Of our faith
Take this pain
With open arms
Open dreams of bliss
You're my charm
Of our faith
Of our faith
In dreams of storm
Kill the song of torn
When we make
When we take.

Yesterday

O dreams there is no turning back
<u>Things</u> could be so godlike simple
But this world is a twisted scheme, love.

(I lost my heart. Yesterday.)

O and we try to find a touch of hope
<u>We</u> look into our children, their eyes.
But this only reveals a lesser version of us.

(I lost my mind. Yesterday.)

O I sought out pain in sex and drugs
<u>Fucked,</u> got fucked, sucked and came.
But this only made me self centered & lazy.

(I lost my soul. Yesterday.)

O careless as we may ever become
<u>Together</u> we may be able to overcome
But first we must be prepared to sacrifice.

(I lost my life. Yesterday.)

Friends

We could have gone so far together
Child, love, we could have crossed oceans
  Of painful retribution together.

Different aisles, different times, together
But always the same… like sadness always
And forever… and forever with tears.

O friend we remain untouchable lovers
We lay on nonexistent sheets of passion & pride
  Of sexual star crossed ecstasy.

I will see you tomorrow when the sun rises
For the horizon is an old man too tired to keep up.
He falls away each day only to await suns return.

I Do Not

I do not love you, my love.
It sounds the way it sounds
But when it comes down to it
No love will ever hold me down.

Indifference

Blaring passions, stirred emotions
I want to become a serial killer
Time to head east into India
Where people (children) disappear
And cops sit back.
30 bodies found, chopped up limbs
In a ditch. Mud. Flesh buried in shit.
It was so intoxicatingly beautiful
As if displayed shock
Across the faces of law enforcement.
Families had searched and today
Their efforts were met with one benefit
They found their children (in pieces).
Imagine being a dignified law enforcer
In front of those incomplete families.
A mother holding an arm
A father clutching a head
Pieces of young boys & girls...
One cop over there apparently found
The answer when he said:
"If you don't want your kids to die, don't have any!"
So god-damned beautiful.

Fallin' Out of Love

We died together
Lovers in an omega
We fucked, forever
Song of bliss
In this
Do me a favor
I have a single wish
We killed the mad dog 'Savor'
And now, understand
Our looted treasure
Is this…
Is no more.

Fool

(I sold my soul to… God!
Fool! We can't sell somethin' we don't own.)

You want to know the truth of it all, father?
Only thing we need love is the creator up above.
He has possession of our souls. He and he alone.

Fabled Damned

One

Allen said something about 'Fabled Damned of Nations'
Walt said something of the sort before him.
Who ever said it, if both said it, does not matter
 What matters, my blood, is the manifestation.

I know the fabled damned of my nation
They live in buildings that touch the heavens
Trudging up through concrete, living with mice
Roaches poured out cereal boxes,
Flicked off, bon a petit. 'Project' buildings
Forty stories tall and home to millions
Drugs on the first floor
Bookies on the second floor
Prostitution on the third and forth floor
Etc, etc, etc…

O sweet blood of mine, I know the fabled damned
Eating out of garbage pails behind every diner
Sleeping in gutters to stay warm
In between two cars for safety
Newspaper for insulation. Yes, my love.
Finding a cup of clean water is jackpot
Dreams flushed down a toilet

In the Virgin Mega store on Time Square
Flushed down the AMC Theater
Flushed down Madam Tussad's wax museum
Here in NYC the fabled damned is U & me.

Two

My brother sent off to die in Bush's mad oil baron war
I miss you, Ishmael. Wherever you are, blind soldier,
If you are gone, heavens above, I will not forgive.
I will resent my nation though you're 'Hero'
This day and age is barbaric is fucking shitty
No one wants to care anymore; no one loves
This day and age shouldn't know murder, war
Anything and ones own self is all that matters.
Ishmael, where the bullets trace the night sky
I love you, my brother. On the 64 squares I await.

Then: my great physical muse cousin Joey
Lost on some mission involving nothing important.
Where are you? Where are your mad taunts?
You use to spew inspiration, just a single
Movement, word, etc… and it was enough
You covered my shadow with firm strength
Showed me, led me to the door of dreams
But cousin where have you gone? I look
And feel sadness… a sadness that speaks
I had to leave my baggage behind.

(Take this how you will.)

You two, Ishmael and Joey, my desires to break free
Of the fabled damned of my nation, our nation.
O the bravery of the soldier
The imagination of the muse
I would have reaped lives for such benefits
Benefits have passed me by here in Democracy.
Fuck Democracy. It doesn't exist.
Ishmael is killing for oil, FOR OIL.
Joey is a man with no purpose.
History will know him not.
They say we're free
But first we have to fill out an application.
I can't shit in my backyard without getting
Ticketed for indecent exposure.
Democracy = whoever has more money (the Bush family)
Decides the outcome of the poor and middle class
Freedom died long ago before any of us lived
Sweet, I know the fabled damned of a nation
It's U & me.

Pit

When I lay on the ground
Run over me and into safety.
Later, with songs of treasured sound
Speak of my heroic sanity, tragedy.

Pit-bull dog came chargin' you
Me and my sadness couldn't see you maimed
I stepped in front of that demon with eyes of blue
And allowed for your escape and my life ending pain.

Rain Water

I watched the rain water flush through the gutter
And I thought of my life and the lives of all others.
The way it rippled through the crevices
Like angels of God offering their services.

Angel lives don't matter. But, the task at hand!
Work ants all for the colony, for their land.
These rain soaked early morning hours in NYC
You'd have to believe in them in order to see.

I Saw My Breath

I saw my breath in the air materialize & fade
A gift of myself to this cold dark city taken away.
What comes of us this world takes with vicious passion
As we attempt our hand at futile expression.

But we can't stop breathing, can't stop existence
If such were so how would you and I have ever known
Our being ever was, ever meant whatever a life
Is ever meant to be, ever could have been?

My name is Doubt. I'm an ancient creature
I rush with many but take my time with many.
My name is Wonder. I'm an ancient lover.
I have rushed all I've touched into insanity.

My Mouth

My mouth hurts
My back is hunched
My minds gone all berserk
O brother I think I'm fucked.

The Rivers of Xibalba

1. The River of Scorpions

I began my search for the city of Xibalba through haze &
smoke
With pill & tab, bag of glue & paint, I found the River of
Scorpions.
Death lay across its borders, bodies lined the shore lines
Warriors and soldiers not quiet ready to be called
champions.

Before attempting to cross the piercing waves
I tediously set up camp that cold jungle night.
The trees in the darkness were filled with demons.
So I slept with my back to the waves and ready to fight.

When some small imp fell from the sky and into the set
fire
He danced in the flames shouting: "Xibalba! Xibalba is
near!"
His voice was tremendous for his gnat-like size, beady
eyes
Eyes that seemed disproportioned and riddled with fear.

"What do you seek, Lone Traveler?" in flaming ecstasy
he cried.

"'Tis not good to lay with back turned on such a river."
Upon my feet and prepared to swat the imp, I gave him silence.
"Aaarrgghh, perhaps the Lone Traveler is no stranger to danger?"

And so I met the great Kukulean, god of the wind
Who stayed with me at the shore for a sunrise.
We spoke for hours; he told me of the rivers beyond
All along listening to the forested demon cries.

"I'll take you to the River of Blood, my friend.
Beyond the great Scorpion, beyond this first obstacle.
And he led me through the River of Scorpions
"I wish you luck, my friend. Xibalba! To see it is a miracle."

Vanishing into the sky from whence he'd come
I could see the overgrown path of my next test
Eyes watched me through the forest all around
And I marched forward, plowing the Xibalban forest.

2. *The River of Blood*

I fought the elements and traveled long and hard
During the night time jungle cold I made fire.
I'd look into the heavens and hope for Kukulean
To return, my friend, the great wind rider.

When up ahead, beyond a line of rotting flesh,
O dark forest edge the River came into view.
Bright red it slithered into a gorge
Forever sorrow, sad sickness, where blood holds true.

The smell of putrid flesh bore pangs of pain into me
And as much as I fought I lost control of my bowels.
I fell to my hands and knees, listening to the flow
Of the river, the caked dirt in my hands felt foul.

"I am Ah Itzam." Said the voice of a young woman
I looked up and beheld a fantastic light, a gorgeous glare
"The sight and smell of my river has broken you."
And my strength returned through the force of her stare.

"What are you?" I asked, dumbfounded by her immunity
To the horrors I couldn't ignore, couldn't recover from.
"I am the water witch. I will take you across the river
of blood for the price of your seed, for a son."

So we made love and there, in the mud, I gave her seed
The heat within her brilliant body burned / singed my
flesh
I smiled at her, lying motionless and exhausted, she
carried me
Across and lay me down on the shore to rest.

When I woke Ah Itzam was gone, with her future son.

But her word had been kept and I was across
I looked now at a desert plain with no road
And realized, as far as I had come, I was now lost.

    3.   The River of Pus

"You're now upon the River of Pus." A brutal man-voice declared
"I am here." And he stood and I could see him through camouflage.
"Who are you?" I asked, dropping to my knees, sweating
His body moved in and out of visibility and he seemed mirage.

"Ahekkeh, the Black Hunter." He bowed. "I will take you through
This river for a small price." And he took from his pocket a knife.
I backed away from him, a terrible wild smell carried
In the wind, death. He approached and I feared for my life.

"A finger and I shall lead you to the crossroads of Xibalba."
Hands balled up fists, a tremendous sweat broke from my brow
Fear tore torturous amounts of hesitation into my heart.

"Hunter of Xibalba, your path is sacrifice. You must decide, now."

And I extended my left hand and looked into the desert
A world of great trials lay in those sand dunes.
After my index finger was taken and I regained consciousness
I heard a great shouting in the wind. "Your suffering voice. Loons."

With fire Ahekkeh closed my wounds and we walked
We walked and I became weary with hunger with thirst.
Suddenly, he stopped, flung his knife into a dune
A creature emerged from the sand dead with the knife in its head.
   "Tonight," Ahekkeh began. "We feast."

And so it was we traveled the River of Pus to the
Crossroads of Xibalba for the span of two moons.
Ahekkeh taught me to survive and hunt, kill to eat
When one night he said: "You are now Hunter. We part soon."

As we came to the edge of the desert I could see the village
"And so it is we part." And he was gone, leaving me to the villagers

A year would pass, the four crossroads were seasons, before
I was prepared to face the next tests:

      The six Great Pit Houses of the city of Xibalba.

Tea

Nothin' like a piping hot cup of tea in sheer blizzard cold.
It's a luxury that fights hypothermia and helps you grow
old.
Warms the frigid paralyzed fingers, sooths the inner core
While the winter wind howls and let's out soul shattering
roar.

I wait for the children to arrive; I have their breakfast.
I'll feed one hundred kids with a revitalized body
They'll eat their waffles with a smile and call me the best
Then I'll cook lunch for three hundred young and hungry.

And I had all this strength bestowed upon me
One cup of that precious elixir, that black tea
Tomorrow, at the start of my painfully frozen morning.
I'll drink five cups and ward off long sleeps coming.

Such Vanity

Such vanity in this wretched world
Selfish, depreciative, wicked vanity.
Man has put into place a ferocious mold
Claiming for him self all and fucking humanity.

Concerned Mother

She came into
The school
With abusive
Intention
Child had
Disobeyed her
Authority and brought
A toy to school.
School
Where knowledge
(Sometimes false)
Is dished out
In scientific
Proportion
Child scientifically
Met mothers hand
With a POP!
Such a smack
Tears…
The first lesson
Of becoming an adult…
The first goodbye
To child.

Who Are We

Who are we to sit and judge
With flesh so intoxicating?
As repulsive as it may be, we love sex.
We love it and it's all we ever want.
Fornication in any position
Clean.
Dirty.
As long & short (clean; dirty) as possible
And when the flesh is no more
Shadows and dust
When flesh has no luster, no hunger
(It bores!) What will become of us?
Masturbation
Infatuation with satisfaction
I want to judge you, my love
I want to kiss the ground you walk on.
And if…
If I should lose interest in you
I will place the barrel in my mouth
And pull the trigger.

Johnny

My cousin Johnny -
My cousin is a faggot -
I love him.
Ask me if I care,
If it at all matters?
He love's men
I love him.
At least he is free.
At least… he is free.

Bush

Bush called for more troops the other day.
He hasn't the ability to 'Talk' peace
He's killed so many with his private war
I begin to wonder when God will intervene.

I am Dreams

I am Dreams, the great demon of snow
Falling from up high, from the unknown
I've loved you like stars in a flow.

Of brilliant green light; blaze & haze
The way I am, with impulsive life, amaze
Me, my love, with songs of how much sleep
Could mean and ever be to me.

I am Dreams, the great demon of snow
Flaked off the scalp of all who know
Where true love is and should forever go.

Today Was For Myself

Today was for myself
And I gave myself to love
O daughter, how you smile!
How you bring such joy
To my mangled heart.

So I missed work
This morning I lived
A moment I shall hold
Forever until…
Yes, my love, I will.

You ran through the aisles
Of 'Toys R Us' and I watched
You are so beautiful
I never want to let go
Never want to be without you.

But time is disgusting
And if I should forget
This poem and what it means
Forgive me, my princess
Forgive an old fool.

Hopeless

You don't know where to go
You don't know where you've been
Lookin' into the sky at night
You don't know where to begin.

Let Me Be

Let me be a revolutionary
Like Neruda
Or Guevera

I want to unite
Like Whitman
Or Frost

Move generations
Like Ginsberg
And Kerouac

I want to stand for my people
Like Hughes
And Angelo

I want to love darkness
Like Blake
Or Poe

I want to be
Anyone but me
How pathetic.

Savage

For Lou

As a child I put you to war with your blood
As a man I respect the father you've become.

Though misfortune may have fucked you hard
Your path shall be lesson for your son

He will look at you, his father, a warrior
He will love your inability to abandon

What you love. And I see, my cousin,
You would murder the world

If it jeopardized a single moments peace
Between you and him. But murder
Doesn't prove love, self sacrifice does.

Josh will look into your eyes
Hug you, kiss you, talk to you
And it will happen, Savage, it will…

You will see it, maybe only for a moment
Maybe two if luck proves the victor
You will see that though your childhood

Burned the hope from your soul
Josh returned it.
Savage!
You gave him life

When the woman who gave him entrance
Abandoned him for freedom
(Though she lost her way)
You preserved him. When darkness

Wanted to swallow him whole
You gave every inch of your body
To stop the tide, to protect him
And he will know this… and not
Because of this poem

But because you will carry him
To the doorstep of his dreams
You will place him higher then you
Your self have ever been.
Dragons will burn the world around you
To ash but you'll never falter.

From the path which has become you
Your Josh!
And there will come a day
He will sit with his children, his spouse
And he will say: "They called my father Savage.

They called him this because he fought for me
Like a lion."

My cousin, I put you to war as a child
And now you're a man I can look up to
You're a father I can feel proud to envy
But you know this already
And if you didn't
Now you do.
In the words of Che:

"Hasta la victoria siempre!"

Mad Son of a Bitch

Everyone
Wants to be
Rich
Famous
Porn star
Heroes.

The greatest benefits to humanity
And they've elected a president,
Twice,
Who was born with 'Mass Murderer' branded
Into his smile.

Rich = only oil baron Bush
Famous = America. A reputation
          for killing entire countries.
Porn Star = who ever dies for a gallon
          of what he wants.
Heroes = everyone who elected that
          Mad son of a bitch.

If you see any benefits from this above
Let me know. I can't see any.

I've Neglected

I've neglected
So much
Time with
You my sweet.
Neglected
So many
Priceless moments
With you.
If God took me
Today into some
Place other then
Here & here
I'd miss you.
I love you.
I'll always
Love you.
If God took me
Today I would
Want you to read
Every word I ever
Wrote down
So I could
Get to know you.

The Weights Go Up

The weights go up and down
Little brother takin' on the rep
Tryin' to be as strong as Satan.

He's enrolled in Hell 144, a junior
High near CO-OP City ghetto.
Where bids of one to five come
With early Christmas burden.

Denial of Me

I will have no success in my life, I know.
I will walk the walk of common man, I know.
And when our dreams fade fast, broken, useless
I'll say to you: "when you saw me smile, you knew."

I Can See the World

I can see the world, again.
Gucci has saved my sight.
I can see the world, again.
O my city shines so bright.

The eye-glass man asked:
"Hard not bein' able to see?"
I paid him five hundred dollars and
Looked into a mirror, found me.

They sat beautiful on my face
Madre said black suits me.
I had to escape that place
Of materialistic tragedy.

My Four Professors

Anne Sexton with the beautiful face
Poetess & lovely, feminist & lonely
I fell in love with you today.
Yesterday I loved Pablo Neruda.
Day before that, Allen Ginsberg.
Always & always, Walt Whitman.
I've made love to each of you
Numerous times. Always. I fell in love
And now I feel as if only you four
Can understand me. But the four
Of you have long gone from this world.
Allen being the last ten years ago.
I look to you four with hope as a student
And know one day I'll be a colleague.

We Woke in the Grass

We woke in the grass
Under a blue sky breeze
Empty forties lying beside us
Us lying beside us.

Viper held his head and seemed
So out on his abused back.
Kenny tried to smile rolled over
Onto his side and back to sleep.

"Let's go to my house." David said,
Getting to his mud covered feet.
A giant dog head emerged
From a combined leaf convergence.

J smiled, stopped quickly
David started vomiting
Viper & Kenny were snoring
I was spinning.

"You guys see the dog?" I asked,
J helping me to my feet.
He was vomit green.
"I think we all saw the dog, brother."
        And he tried to smile.

She Never Showed

She said she had fallen on hard times
No cash and only one minimum wage part-time

For support with a boyfriend on a disability
And enticed by the sweet hydro-hemp fiend

Once a month with dreams no where in sight
I called a friend, a brother, that very night

Got her a waitress position with a seconds time
She won the interview with a great horse smile

First day of work she never showed
Then she wonders the sadness of her situation

When she hasn't the determination
To fight for a better existence

After Four Days

After four days of relaxation I return to hell
O the beginnings of yearned for vacation
The disappointment of dreaded conclusion.

I Make My Own

For Clark

And, my brother, how I was overjoyed
      When you visited us.
How I wanted to take you in my arms
      And ask how you've been.
Your son and daughter with my daughter
      Your telling me you can stay long
I cook you a hot dog
      It's not much in way of food.
Some for your children.
      My friend, she your daughter
Like the turning of wine
      She has a tinge of ex-wife.
Blood of blood of blood
      I fear for her in what future she may win
I fear for you because her win is your loss.
      And your loss brings joy to ex-wife.
O ask me why I should care, my brother
      Ask me to cry for coming existence
I will.
      She's my daughters friend
Your daughter
      I love her like I love my own
Your son is my son
      Such is such

I would kill and be killed for yours
>
> But yes she's my daughters friend, sister

And what is it that flourishes within her

> Can one day flourish in mine.

You see now my fear.

> My daughter can become your ex being
>
> Friends with your daughter who has already
>
> Become your ex.

But, Brother, I can never rid my self of you

> I love you and the three of you

B,B,B!

> And so the baggage you carry I make my own

O how I was overjoyed, today

> When you visited us.

Multiple Sclerosis

Multiple sclerosis and I remember you, my Julia.
Long nights of card games filled laughter on smoke.
Jell-O shots and Virginia Slims all night like love
And we never wanted it to end, Julia. Never-ever!

Multiple sclerosis and TV with Chinese food.
Eddie would sit and draw boats in 2-D
Kay would argue about everything and Eddie
And then Tony. Horror! How I loved Tony!

Classic Dracula with a twist of Wolfman
Frankenstein on Lost Boys with a side of Elvira.
Night of the Living Dead and I believed you.
Freddy and Jason; Leprechaun and Chucky.
     All night… all night… all night…

You'd laugh, Julia. You'd tell Mom & Dad I was old enough
"Not to worry!" Horror. It' just a card game
A Jell-O shot, multiple sclerosis and death on a t-shirt.
She loved so much I believe hate resented her
     Almond shaped eyes.

I kissed her cheek when last we parted.
I kissed her I kissed her I kissed them all

O I knew I'd never see her again, them again
Multiple sclerosis and Peekskill and back to the Bronx.

They say when she died: Multiple Sclerosis
Pulled an ace and king in a wicked fifty hand game
Of all night Jell-O shot blackjack.
I remember you, Julia. My love 2nd grandma.

Eddie and your 2-D boats I loved you.
Kay and your argumentation I loved you.
Tony and your library of classic horror VHS I loved you
O how I still dream of your places in my childhood.

Multiple Sclerosis may have separated us, scattered
Us to the winds but my memories of you all
Will remain forever until…

It's Freezing

It's freezing and dark morning outside.
Cold like this and stars are afraid to shine.
Left the house this morning right on time,
Left my two ladies in bed snoring.

Vero said: "Joe, put Isis back in her bed."
(My throat hurts. I think I'm getting sick.)
"No, Vero." I whispered.

"The warmest place is beside you."

And she pulled Isis, snoring-sleeping-Isis,
Into her arms and under the quilt.
(O how I wanted to lie beside the two of them.)

I zippered up and went to work alone
In the freezing and dark morning
Cold like this and stars…
Stars are afraid to shine.

Life Is So

Life is so fuckin' fucked
Fuckin' shitty and terrible.
But death isn't appealing
(Can't have sex dead)

I stabbed myself in my leg with a pen
Wrote this poem in blood.

I wanted it to resemble life.

There's a Vicious

There's a vicious
Infection in my blood.
Last night
Body aches, throat
Pains I suffered.

I blew my nose
To no benefit.
Showered
Cleansed with no effect.
Vero said:

"You could be
Dying."
But she's only
Playing
(I hope).

So Strong

For my friend, Toni Q. Long

Yeah
You were so strong
When the devil came to brake you down.
I sat there
Listening to the devil spit at you.
The devil in a form
(Child today-murderer tomorrow).
Nothin' we could do,
You could do,
Simply sorrow-tragic.

I love your patience with the devil.
How you spoke your heart
Against the devil.
The devil in a form
(demon today-hell bound always).
When the devil came
With shit filled slander…
When the devils eyes
Glared with ice cold fire…
When the persecution
Of you seemed to be
The devils outlet…

I love you, my friend.
Though that demon wants you
More then many can be had,
I love you.

devil came out of the gutter
devil in the walls of your cubicle
devil in the words of those who've forgotten their
beginnings
devil laughing hard in forms of envy
devil and you, Toni, shout out "Jesus loves me!"
devil and I say "FUCK YOU, devil!"

devil or not you must be tired.
As I sat there listening
Knowing I would have failed
The trial you had overcame
I wanted to cry
For your superb dignity.

I haven't the courage
To walk your road, my friend.

But to see you... to see your faith
Your hope,
Your glory,
Your desire in divine verse,
Your eyes of experienced pain.

I am restored with belief
I am restored with Christ.

Thank you, sister… my sister
I love you
Like a lost soul
Looking up into a heaven
He'll never know.

First Snow

First snow fall Jan. 18, 2007 and I'm sick.
Sky gray with clouds all mingled (shit-blended)
People have astonishment flaked into their faces.
Snow!
Snow!
"Is it real?" they ask, never having seen snow
(Well, the type of astonishment they suffered
led me to believe they'd never seen snow).
"O it's cold!"
"O it's on my nose!"

Chest feels congested.
My nose doesn't work
It keeps running mucus snow flake: Mucus-Mucus
And when it stops: more Mucus.

O here we are in Einstein Radiology
EKG not for me but Vero.
Don't question the purpose of the x-ray
It's like snow falling. Vero's foot hurts
I think that's why the Doc's
Want to x-ray her chest.

Polished floors and changing rooms
I CAN'T BREATHE!

Too many Doc's   too many dieing people
On gurneys with tears and death.

And Vero put on a robe to cover her chest,
Her bare chest.
Cold Einstein.
Cold me.

Her nipples show through the wrinkled blue robe
I can't breathe but something in my pants…
O she's the type of attraction that excites,

Paralyzes!
Makes me wish I felt some kind of better.

"Are x-rays necessary?" she asks.
"They're like snow flakes." I answer.
And look out of the waiting room
Sign on the wall: Radiology.
Radiology!
Something about this word makes me think radioactive.
Radioactive x-rays.
Radioactive dieing people at Einstein.
Radioactive Vero real soon.

The snow looks so terrible in the drift.
It has made the world a painting of black and white
Frame of radioactive insurance card.

I still can't breathe.
Free thinking people!
Call it radioactive bullshit.
I hope it'll still be snowing
When we get out of this
Beeping hell of feces
The orderly just passed me
With feces covered bed sheets in hand
Feces on wall, tiled floor… shiny tiled floor.
Radioactive feces.

Beep Beep Beeeeeeeeeeeeeeeeeeeeeeeeeeeeeeep!
Someone's machine trying to tell someone
That someone is dead.
I think I should get a beeping machine.
Beep.
False alarm.
Beep!
I could stuff it up my ass.

O Doc just took my Vero.
When she comes back to me
She'll have a radioactive glow
She'll turn the falling snow,
The gang raped world radioactive.
My hair will fall out.

(That's a good thing in terms of never

having to shave that pesky crap from
my face. Face. Feces.)

She's back! Two minutes and she's back
She's not green yet but she's back.

Well, it's off to the snow and out of this hell
But, before I forget, first things first.
First, I have got to get one of those
Annoying beeping machines for
My ass.

My Desire to Strive

My desire to strive for better has gone omega
Omega = close your eyes and embrace the darkness.
Plug up your ears and consume the silence
Cut off your hands & feel existence.

Omega the stars have always been
All that's ever mattered more then here.
We fucked until our legs were omega
My soul no longer satisfied in my scrotum.

My soul had been freedom with sigh and bliss
An exception through lips (cosmos) and ass.
Omega without sex and the body has no use
Omega with sex and life is what I choose.

Broken Conceptions

I love you with broken conceptions of alcohol
I love you like soiled Kotex on kitchen floor.
We're the shot out stains on walls
Names of prostitutes carved into doors.

Man stopped me in park God knows when
Offered me in my youth free sex for free.
I declined being that I'm heterosexual man
And homosexual isn't my cup of tea.

When I got home from my walk
Stripped to the nude and called Vero.
After a small unimportant talk
We fucked and I forgot that park convo.

Fresh Coat

There was a fresh coat of snow
Over the face of New York City.

Walking through the purity of it
Avoiding the footprint imprints of previous

I fell in love with my city borough, again.
The Bronx on an MTA bus with Southern Sun

As loud as it could be in my ears
The first snow melting on my brow.

O clouds you have made the world
And all its inhaditants on this day

All one color.
All one faith.
All with a single layer of snow.
All and omega is…
All and omega is no more.
All the Fuck-you's are replaced
        With extra awareness.

People, now, are willing to be people.
Yes, and help a stranger in need.

Man falls onto knees: shouts in pain.
No 'fuck you' today

Today the many stop to help.
Today with a single layer of snow,

Snow forgotten with a years time
Self sacrifice of time for another,

Another not known is remarkable
And with a few seconds time
The snow fall and every step made
Every walking entity of this wretched

Dark, but today white, city
Is taken with a sense of crisp freshness.

I love waking
With fresh a fresh coat of wintry snow

I Saw My Brother

I saw my brother, today.
Homeless and wrapped in a filthy quilt
Walking and riding the subway tunnels
In the freeze of NYC.

I looked into his face
But he didn't know me.
My clothes are clean, his soiled.
My body has been washed, his soiled.

I sleep in a bed under a roof and heat.
He sleeps wherever sleep maybe had
His shoes are riddled with holes
Mine are new… Nike Air.

I tried to tell him I love him.
But he refused to recognize me.
When I took from my pocket
$ 1.00.

His attention was bought and I smiled
"Brother?" I began.
"Yes?" he complied.
"We walked the same path

For God knows how long.
I went one way,
You went the other.
But, our blood, my brother,

Is the gift of omega, the same.
Where you are
I have often dreamt of being.
Instead, I have useless responsibility.

And you have complete freedom.
I envy you.
This is where my love derives,
This envy."

I give him the $.
He accepts
And we continue on
Our separate ways.

Broken, Forever (Prelude)

Broken, forever on a carpet of dreams
Kiss me, fool, and repair what I no longer want.
Omega my song of life suffering& fatigue.
Sloth on my loins and lips.
My lungs have ruptured, have torn open,
        No longer work.

I've seen gifts of sanctuary melt away
Dissolved & nothing.
I've seen the broken, forever on my face
Through a mirror of shit.
I resemble myself to such form!

Would you
Through this resemblance
Love me would you kiss me
O, I, this broken, forever,
I would you if you were me and I you.

Padre

Father…
I miss your laugh.
But as much as I want you in my life
Father… I can't forget your wrath.

Satan in My Love

O there are times I see Satan in my love
Satan burning down Fordham Road and its stores.
He's there playing dice, cheatin' the ignorant.
He's there sellin' dreams in ounces on corners.
I know this because I'm ignorant and have dreams.

Flesh for sale in back street gutters
Dirty mattress on roof top for fucking
Pure Decatur Avenue fucking.
Lookin' for death at or around my love.
Try the Grand Concourse, where you're sure
To catch that very special bus.
Boomp!

And you'll be first class into the gates!
(Heaven? Hell? Which ever you're sure of.)

The great Fordham Road in the Bronx of NYC
Built on a fault line and surrounded by ghetto
Populated by ghetto people with bling-bling
And stories of how they've been forsaken
The great Fordham Road...

Spray painted "Mass Graveyard" of the decades.
From Webster Ave. to Roosevelt High entrance

Into the South Bronx, where Satan himself lives.

Car accidents.
Exploding stores.
HIV victims selling cell phones.
High school drop-outs selling outer space,
I love this place.

I was once pick-pocketed here
And ever since that bloody day
I've been in love.

I Don't Want You to Cry

I don't want you to cry, my love.
Never do, never want you to fret.
But you can't get away with hitting people.
You can't abuse your youth,
Take advantage of adults using love.

(But you're so beautiful!)
Yes, and if I were without you I don't
Know where my life would be.
And my little heart I give to you
Everything I am, everything I ever do…

What I am, if you should desire, is yours.
But, you can't take advantage of people
My love, not with violence
Or curled lower lip threats
Of love replaced with hatred.

New Restaurants

Nothing like eating
In a new restaurant
Food unique and delicious.
Crisp workers in ironed uniforms
Polite and lovely for the first two weeks
Spotless and obedient for the first two weeks.

Then: Paycheck.

And hell has come home.
The shit has hit the fan.
Politeness turns wrath
Spotless turns sloth
And what was once delicious
Becomes tainted and tragic.

Today: The Grand Opening.

I have thirteen days
To eat healthy
Clean and well prepared
Food.
After that there's no telling
What will be in my plate and
        Who it came from.

I've Given You My Sickness

I've given you my sickness involuntarily with love.
I didn't mean for this, sweet stars on lips.
Happened how it happened and I was glad when it did.
Glad 'cause I see now you're no better then I.
Held you up in high regards like Satan or Christ.

But with each sneeze there's clarification.
You're human like I and I'm satisfied.
In the mirror we're omega
To the x-ray neither
Of us know any better.

I am dreams (so are you).
I am pain (so are you).
I am life (so are you).
Brothers & sisters we are
And no better.

Cough!
Cough!
Aachu!
Aachu!
God bless you!

Endless Crap

Endless crap eaten off lollipop sticks
Words mingling, fucking, right off your lips.
Sewer pipe toss salad eaten at a buffet.
Herpes covered flesh donuts at the Sabbath.

Cock-dogs and pig feet movie theater
Cunt tacos splashed with hot sauce flavor.
Gluttonous colonic of everyday sadness
A gift of 'fuck you' added to the madness.

(I don't want to tell you I love you 'cause I love you
don't want to don't cause I don't want to.)
Chicken wings smothered in feces and crap
Love, for Valentines Day I got you a marinated rat.

Bon a petit.

WAR

At work they talked
Of youth killed
In war.

I thought of my brother,
Ishmael
At war.

I asked myself
If he's still
Alive.

Lookin' for an answer,
Nauseated,
I left work.

Didn't want to think
About it.
Didn't want to understand
War
Anymore.

Why a man of twenty-six
had to become a savage
for the government he was

born to?

(Turn into a pigeon.   W = worthless
Nothin' fancy,   A = and
Just an old pigeon   R = ridiculous
On Pelham Parkway.
Fly off into the sunset
Spread my hippie wings
And head west.)

Alarm Clock

Alarm clock didn't wake me today
Slept right on through the beeping
Madre woke me with light tapping
At around when I was supposed

To have been left by fifteen minutes.
I leapt from our bed in a great hurry.
Showered / dressed / demanded
"Vero, give me cash for a taxi!"

She didn't have any cash.
Madre gave me the cash
After she called a taxi for me.
Madre woke me; called a taxi

And she paid for it.
While in the limo and then arriving
At work three minutes early, I thought:
'Does Madre love me? Or did she just
        Want to get rid of me?'

Woke This Mornin'

Woke this mornin'
To a white mornin'
Snow covered NYC
An ivory blanket
Of blizzard
Dreams.
A great end
To an even greater
Night.

Vero woke,
Her pajama pants
Missing.
Naked: waist down.

In the dark
Of early mornin' freeze
She asks me
What happened over
Night?

"I took them off of you!"
I answer, smiling
Teeth glaring in the
Darkness.

"Why?"

And as she fell back into
Dreams
And I prepared
For a days work
The dark night fall
Consuming our
Flesh
The room smelling
Of our sex
I spoke aloud:
"I just wanted to
Make sure it was you."

Twice Over

She looked at me twice over
This young beauty of beauty.
I would have felt great urgency
If not married.

At home I have every book
Written by James Clavell
Except one
It was in the hands of beauty
It was in her hands
And I just let her go.

Thank You

For Clara Sala

It's been eight years
Since I took that workshop.
Tryin' to write a novel
Tryin' to be a poet.
The class was held
In some shabby library
But I think
You would have held
My attention anywhere
Then: I wanted to be
What you were & are,
Poet.

You gave us
Your little lessons.
We completed around
Ten trial poems
& earned the title:
'Summer Stars'.
But this is trivial
And though I fell
Away from poetry
For many years

I never forgot you,
Ms. Sala.

Alcohol swept me away
But I kept your words
"Keep practicing and when
You're my age you'll be
Incredible."
And you smiled.
Beautiful poetess, you smiled.

We lose ourselves
Across the streams of time.
It's natural.
Painful as it may be
I wanted to hold on
But I wasn't ready.

And then it was you
Standing over me
Poetess!
Lovely god-like poetess!
Sister.
My sister,
I wanted to tell you
How I loved you.

You planted a poet's seed
In me so long ago
Ages it feels like
And it still lives.
I use it everyday
With hope
With my toothbrush
At work
In dreams

Clara, thank you!

With kisses of unsung bliss
Passion on a page and in lesson
God gave you to me for a mere moment
And your gift of poem will flourish
Because, this time, I won't let it
Die!

Below

It's about five below here in the Big Apple
Five below and you forget how to talk.
Five below and your fingers become stone
Remnants of once was poet.

My frozen breath reminds me of life
The chilled marrow of my bones
Speaks of omega days.
O in my youth I bore the cold.

Now, ebbing upon my thirties
Five below and rigamortis sets in
Face falls off
Face falls off

This is why NYC winters are
So frost-bitingly precious
It drives a force of remembrance
Into our souls,

A remembrance
Of sweated flesh
Of summer breeze
Of boiled nights

In the city of lights
Aaaaarrrggghhh!
But it's five below!
It's five below!

The NYC Cop

Flashin' red & whites on white & blue
People,
Citizens move in fear, move in hesitation
There are guns involved
Men with power trips called Law.
Here in NYC these officers of order
Bring the pain.
Call 'em murderers, killers, merc's
Here in NYC you don't question five-O
You'll catch 41 shots in the chest
Without remorse without care.
The 'Mad Plunger' squad
Take care your anus…
Leave you a forced enema.

No, there's honesty; loyal officers.
It's just their all promoted to DT's
And demons walk the streets in their stead.
Terrorizing the innocent
Taking livelihoods.

(Can you say you're grateful?
Can you say their presence doesn't spark fear?)

Law is justice

The criminal fears justice.

Five-O and everything is in fear.

Mom…

Dad…

Cat…

Goldfish…

Deep treacherous fear.

Flashin' red & whites on white & blue

Run as fast as you can and don't ever-

Ever look back.

Drunk

And my dreams escape
In savage whispers of mourning
Escape me and flee
Into common crevices of frailty.

Great orgasmic song
Of pleasure on a broken floor.
I've given too much of my life
My damned soul to a bottle.

O if help were accurate
And pride absent of form
How'd I dream of life upon
My feet and ready to face the world
        Sober.

The Great Bukowski

Last night
Bukowski
Gave me a lesson
In the beauty
Of free verse
And
I fell head over heels.
His flow
Feel
Beer
Cigarettes
Gambling
Fuck
Life was so enticing,
So like my own.
But he tells it better.

I read into the AM
Running
My fingers over
Every page
Trying to love
Every word written
By that beer
Gut poet

Classic / modern master.

In the mirror
My stomach
Resembles his.
Vero rolls her eyes
At me. She hates
When I look in the mirror.
"You're not fat, Joe." She says.
"No!" I put both hands
on my belly.

"All you got is a beer belly."
"Oh."
"I hate that about you."
"What?"
"Last week you wanted a beard
Like Whitman.
The week before that
You wanted to kill yourself
Like Sexton.
Now, you got a beer belly
Like Bukowski."

"They say Ginsberg was
Homosexual."

"Leave me alone, crazy!"

So I do
And
We sleep.

A Need for More

I feel like I'm falling
Off of this practice.
I don't want this
To become sloppy seconds.
Terrible ways I carry
About myself, in myself
Vacation is the cure
And salvation is soon.

This ain't no Leap year
But February is February
And I got a whole week
Off somewhere
In there I'll find
Some time to breath
Air & patience
And this art form.

Maybe, if there's enough time
I can plan something.
Make reservations
At a hotel in Manhattan.
Vero would enjoy that
And so would poetry
No more useless thoughts.

The Cold

The cold does wonders on flesh
Inside and, fuckin', outside too.
Every soul layered up and ready for it.
Why? Cold is pain and pain is pure.
No one wants to be pure.
(As if purity were overrated.)
I like the cold
It helps me think
Helps me be poet.
Poet!

Child!

Child!
My lovely child.
When you see your parents again
Tell them you love them,
Tell them you've learned
How hard life can be.

Flesh...

Flesh... you desire
You'd trade all your possessions
For a slice.
For a wrinkle in time.
"I devoured every square inch of
sexual appetite." You'd say
on your death bed.
"Sex
was all it was ever about.
Flavor.
Being a predator of
Panties / blood / yeast and
Pubic realms."

The Pimp

"I guarantee blood on your shit
when you finish with this one."
He started to sell me his game.
"Look,"
rubbing at his goatee
"You're a consistent customer.
Never a problem.
Here's my proposal, and
Don't forget this is fresh
Ass we're talkin' 'bout here,
A single favor."

Is anyone in a position
To sell their soul
To the devil?
How do you sell something
That belongs to God?
I wasn't hesitant
Towards action
Felt no fear towards
An unknown future.
He tossed in the word:
"Hunger!"
and yes, it was hunger.
A blind hunger

For satisfaction of desire.
I worked harder
To accomplish my goals
When hungry…
Craving.

"How long will I have her?"
holding strong eye contact.
This was important.
Alpha male power play
Time

If my soul was for sale
Then let the collection of it
Be the furthest thing from the
Now.
"I want an entire night!"
"Fuck, man." He started pacing
"Look…
$500
and a favor. She's yours
tonight. All night."

Fresh ass!
Brand new off the plane.
Could any hungry soul refuse?
Could I refuse?
Goose flesh waved over

My chest
And I knew such offers were rare.
Fresh ass!
Brand new ass!
Smiling I answered:
"There better be blood on my shit!"
and he said:
"Try not to kill
the merchandise."

Another human being.
Merchandise.
Fresh ass merchandise.

The Child Prostitute

Tears
From a fifteen year old
Prostitute. Weeping; pain.
These things,
Actions of emotion,
They can have momentous effect.

Oceans can dry into deserts
Stars can fade out of the night sky.
You look forward into tomorrow…
But see only sorrow.
Sorrow can make you look at life
With a vicious perspective.

What you are,
The dead-set definition
You held tightly of yourself,
Can be proven wrong.
This sorrow can have you
Questioning the meaning of everything
You thought
you were sure of.

The Escape

She sat up
Ignoring her slight pain.
It's amazing how good fortune
Can drive you to ignore
Pain.

She watched me dressing
Listened to the rustle of
My khaki pants being slid
Up to my waist the buckling
Of my leather belt.

There was something so appealing
In a man preparing to face
The world having enough determination
To step into a void of
Darkness & Decision.

"Are you serious about this?" she asked,
her small breasts pointed with youth.
I had moments ago known
Those breasts kissed them listened
To the beating heart behind them.

Smiling flesh merging in kiss

I answered her with lust:
"To make a mistake is easy.
To realize, understand, and correct...
That takes courage."

No Sympathy

There's no sympathy here
No charm in my eyes
No rose petals on my soul
No sudden conceptions of omega
No twinklin' moments of masturbation
Cum shots on images of anorexia.

Fuck the sensation of alcohol
Fuck the weed da blunt da dro.
No false pretense
Not a sign of common sense
Omega days twirled up into heaven
Hell claims the trimmings.

Hell is our song
No love in this heart
No compassion or intrest.
Saw the sun set, rise, and set again.
My insurance doesn't cover insanity
So I'm not insane.

I wanna say good-bye
Tell you thanks for your time
But I'm a New Yorker
So I'll cut this short… Bellevue Style:

"Fuck you! I don't want no donut and
the elephant in my toilet tied my shoes."

O My Blessed Lord

O my blessed lord
O my blessed lord
I've loved you since the day I was born
And if ever I leave your side
To walk the road of pride
O my blessed lord
Remain my guide.

You gave your son to us
Now in you, Lord, we trust
O my blessed lord
I fight my lust.
Through this sin
And so much strife
I walk the road of life
O my blessed lord
Remain my guide.

My Pops

My Pops on some rage broke my face
And as I fell... I fell with a swan's grace.
Layin' there this pitiful child in the wild
Back then defendin' myself wasn't my style.

God-damned! If I hadn't been so small, so weak
I would have taken a pipe and broke his knees.
That was way back when. Shit, I was just ten
Feelin' like a welfare token born because pops
Forgot his Trojan.

Rebirth

My girl told me to try and see
The beauty in life
But I got this alcoholic hunger
That's waitin' for me to die.

Goin' to work now   livin'
Life as my own man
Getting' with these flash
Backs of my fathers hand.

Visions of jumpin'
In front of a train
To drown my pain
Eats up my mind
And all I can see
Is his terrible crime.

Abused, but like Christ
I know how to forgive
Now, with open eyes
Love & pride I'm ready
        To live.

My Hands

My hands made love to the page
And my words spoke to you omega
Omega omega omega omega omega
But it doesn't end here, my love.
You and I will go on through the
Gates of Xibalba or the nozzle of a bottle
My sweet reader… I will always love you.

My hands made love to the page
And your eyes made love to my words
O sweet reader in stars of now
Dreams never forgotten, always there
I finish this poem with a kiss
And hope you've learned something
Anything worth learning.

Good night…
Sweet dreams.

www.ingramcontent.com/pod-product-compliance
Lightning Source LLC
LaVergne TN
LVHW011224080426
835509LV00005B/303